RAINBOW OF ANIMALS

WHY ARE ANIMALS PURPLE?

Melissa Stewart

Series Literacy Consultant:
Allan A. De Fina, PhD
Dean, College of Education/Professor of Literacy
Education, New Jersey City University
Past President of the New Jersey Reading Association

Series Science Consultant:
Helen Hess, PhD
Professor of Biology
College of the Atlantic
Bar Harbor, Maine

Contents

Words to Know

attract (uh TRAKT)—To make interested.

blend in—To match; to look the same as.

poison (POY zun)—A material that makes an animal sick. Sometimes the animal gets so sick that it dies.

predator (PREH duh tur)—An animal that hunts and kills other animals for food.

prey (PRAY)—An animal that is hunted by a predator.

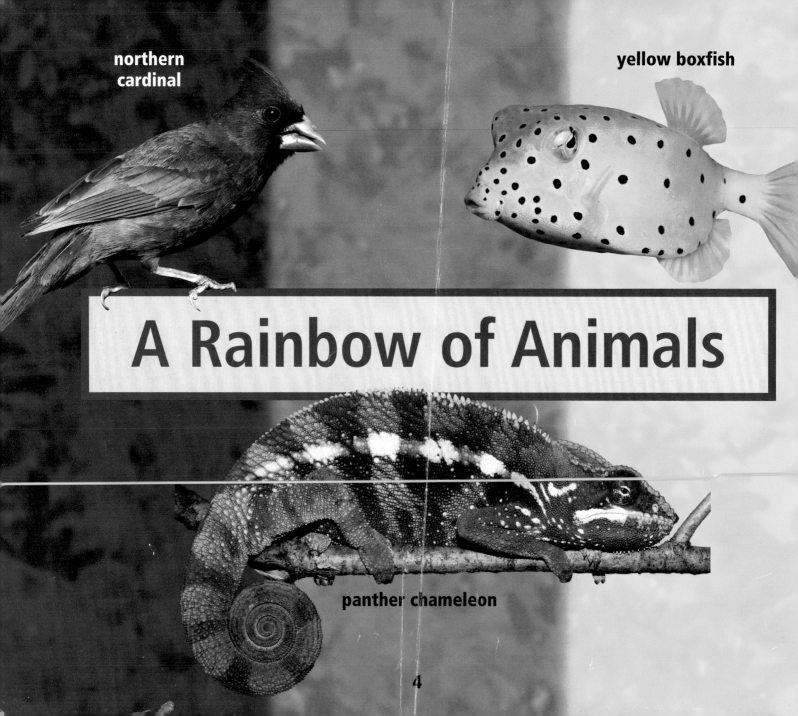

northern cardinal

yellow boxfish

A Rainbow of Animals

panther chameleon

poison dart
frog

Go outside and look around. How many kinds of animals do you see? Dogs and birds are animals. So are insects and fish.

Animals come in all sizes and shapes. And they come in all the colors of the rainbow.

leaf-mimic katydid

lesser purple
emperor butterfly

Purple Animals Near You

    Can you think of some purple animals that live near you? Some birds are purple. So are some insects and spiders.

    Purple animals live in other parts of the world too. Let's take a look at some of them.

Purple Heron

Being purple helps some animals hide. When a heron stands still, it **blends in** with its grassy home. That helps it stay safe from enemies.

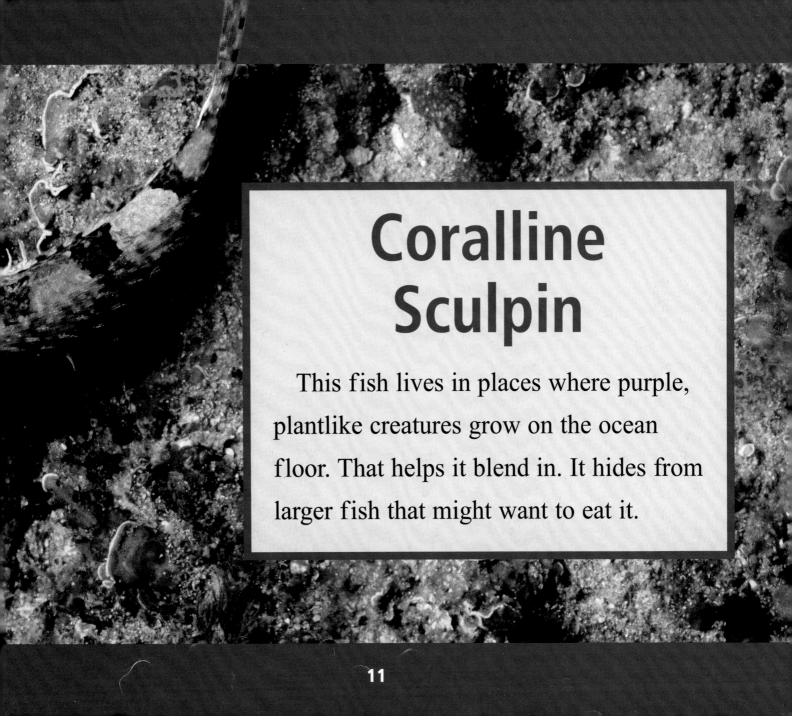

Coralline Sculpin

This fish lives in places where purple, plantlike creatures grow on the ocean floor. That helps it blend in. It hides from larger fish that might want to eat it.

Crab Spider

This spider hunts smaller insects and spiders. It has no trouble catching its **prey** by surprise. It can turn yellow, purple, orange, pink, or white. That way it always matches the flower it is on. Prey cannot see it.

Crowned Wood Nymph

Sometimes being purple helps an animal stand out. This bird's bright body is easy to spot. It helps him **attract** a mate. The female's feathers are green. That helps her hide from **predators** while she sits on her eggs.

Purple Emperor Butterfly

This male butterfly's bright body sends a message to other males. It says, "Stay away. This is my home." The other males know they need to find somewhere else to live.

Agama Lizard

Most lizards live alone, but this male is part of a large group of lizards. His colorful skin lets the other lizards know that he is the boss.

Nudibranch

This sea slug lives in the ocean. It may be small, but it is easy to spot. Its bright colors say, "Leave me alone." If a hungry hunter takes a bite, it will be sorry. A sea slug's body is full of **poison**.

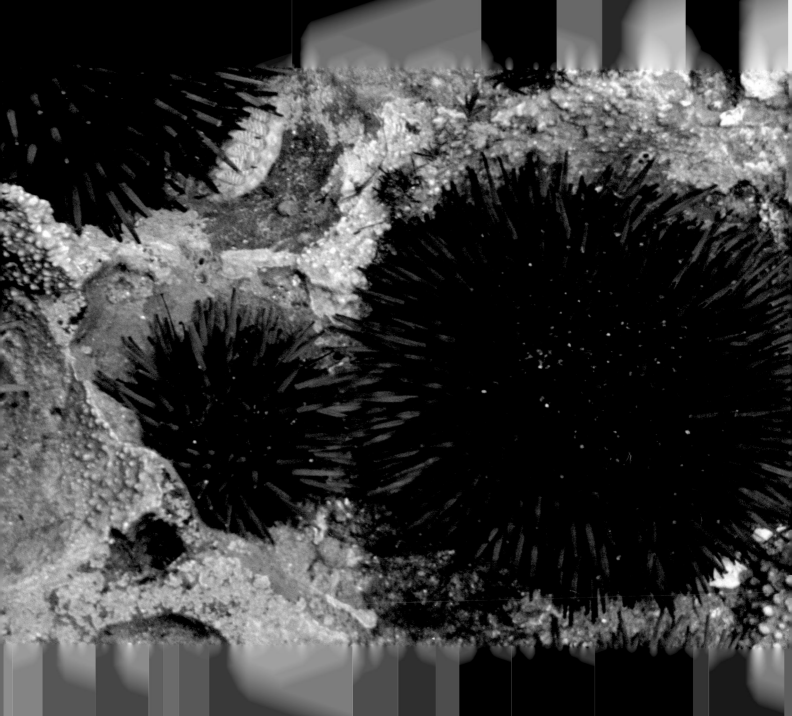

Purple Sea Urchins

Sea urchins make a tasty treat for some ocean animals. But most do not go near them. Predators know that a sea urchin's long spines give a painful prick.

California Sea Hare

A sea hare lives in the ocean too. But it has a different way of staying safe. It sprays its enemies with purple ink. That is enough to send away most predators.

Guessing Game

purple stinger sea jelly

Being purple helps many kinds of animals stay alive in the world. It helps some animals send a message to mates or predators. It helps other animals hide from their enemies. How do you think being purple helps the animals in these photos?

(See answers on page 32.)

Animals Live?

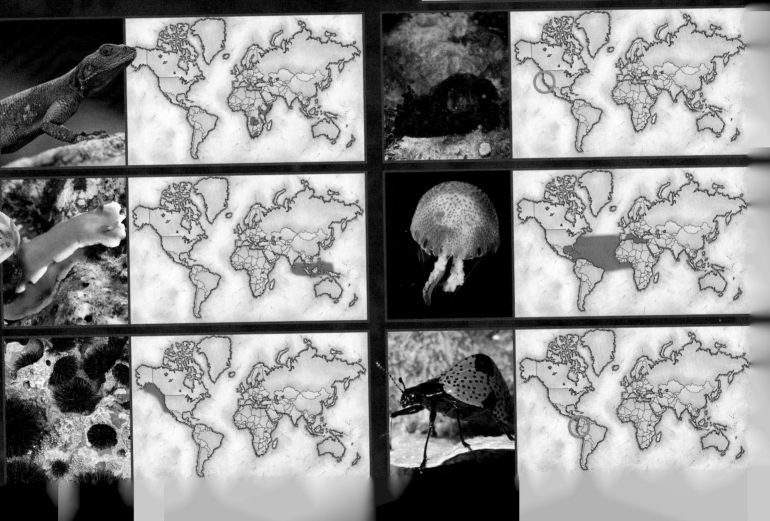

Learn More

Books

Arnosky, Jim. *I See Animals Hiding*. New York: Scholastic, 2000.

Jenkins, Steve. *Living Color*. Boston: Houghton Mifflin, 2007.

Kalman, Bobbie, and John Crossingham. *Camouflage: Changing to Hide*. New York: Crabtree Publishing, 2005.

Stockland, Patricia. *Red Eyes or Blue Feathers: A Book About Animal Colors*. Minneapolis: Picture Window Books, 2005.

Whitehouse, Patricia. *Colors We Eat: Purple and Blue Foods*. Chicago: Heinemann, 2004.

Learn More

Web Sites

Animal Colors
http://www.highlightskids.com/Science/Stories/SS1000_
animalColors.asp

Beasts Playground: Camouflage Game
http://www.abc.net.au/beasts/playground/camouflage.htm

How Animal Camouflage Works
http://animals.howstuffworks.com/animal-facts/animal-
camouflage.htm

Index

Enslow Elementary, an imprint of Enslow Publishers, Inc.

Enslow Elementary® is a registered trademark of Enslow Publishers, Inc.

Copyright © 2009 by Melissa Stewart

Library of Congress Cataloging-in-Publication Data

Stewart, Melissa.
    Why are animals purple? / Melissa Stewart.
        p. cm. — (Rainbow of animals)
    Includes bibliographical references and index.
    Summary: "Uses examples of animals in the wild to explain why some animals are purple"—Provided by publisher.
    ISBN 978-0-7660-3254-5
    1. Animals—Color—Juvenile literature. 2. Purple—Juvenile literature. I. Title.
QL767.S748 2009
591.47'2—dc22   2008011473

ISBN-10: 0-7660-3254-X

Printed in the United States of America

10 9 8 7 6 5 4 3 2 1

To Our Readers: We have done our best to make sure all Internet Addresses in this book were active and appropriate when we went to press. However, the author and the publisher have no control over and assume no liability for the material available on those Internet sites or on other Web sites they may link to. Any comments or suggestions can be sent by e-mail to comments@enslow.com or to the address on the back cover.

Enslow Publishers, Inc., is committed to printing our books on recycled paper. The paper in every book contains 10% to 30% post-consumer waste (PCW). The cover board on the outside of each book contains 100% PCW. Our goal is to do our part to help young people and the environment too!

Every effort has been made to locate all copyright holders of material used in this book. If any errors or omissions have occurred, corrections will be made in future editions of this book.

Interior: Minden Pictures: © Barry Mansell/npl, p. 5 (frog); © Chris Newbert, p. 4 (boxfish); © Do Van Dijck/Foto Natura, pp. 8–9, 28 (heron); © Eddy Marissen/Foto Natura, pp. 1 (bottom left), 22–23, 29 (urchins); © Francis Abbott/npl, pp. 26, 29 (sea jelly); © Frans Lanting, p. 5 (katydid); © Hans Cristoph Kappel/npl, pp. 5 (butterfly), 16–17, 28 (butterfly); © Konrad Wothe, pp. 12–13, 28 (spider); © Michael & Patricia Fogden, pp. 1 (top left, top right), 14–15, 27, 28 (wood nymph), 29 (beetle); © Norbert Wu, pp. 20–21, 24–25, 29 (nudibranch, sea hare); © Pete Oxford, p. 4 (chameleon); © Tom Vezo, pp. 4 (cardinal), 6–7, 28 (martins).
© Bernard Castelein/naturepl.com, pp. 1 (bottom right), 18–19, 29 (lizard); © Jeff Rotman/naturepl.com, pp. 10–11, 28 (fish).

Cover (clockwise from top left): © Michael & Patricia Fogden; © Michael & Patricia Fogden; © Bernard Castelein/naturepl.com; © Eddy Marissen/Foto Natura/Minden Pictures.

Illustration Credits: © 1999, Artville, LLC, pp. 28–29 (maps).

Note to Parents and Teachers: The *Rainbow of Animals* series supports the National Science Education Standards for K–4 science. The Words to Know section introduces subject-specific vocabulary words, including pronunciation and definitions. Early readers may need help with these new words.

Answers to the Guessing Game:

At night, the pale colors of a purple stinger sea jelly blend into its watery world.

The purple body of a fungus beetle warns predators to stay away. If an enemy attacks, it will be sorry. The little insect will let out a bad smell.

Enslow Elementary
an imprint of
Enslow Publishers, Inc.
40 Industrial Road
Box 398
Berkeley Heights, NJ 07922
USA
http://www.enslow.com